Kama Pootra

52 **Mind-Blowing Ways to Poop**

Daniel Cole Young

sourcebooks

Published by Sourcebooks, Inc.
P.O. Box 4410, Naperville, Illinois 60567-4410
(630) 961-3900
Fax: (630) 961-2168
www.sourcebooks.com

Library of Congress Cataloging-in-Publication Data

Young, Daniel Cole.
 Kama pootra : 52 mind-blowing ways to poop / by Daniel Cole Young.
    p. cm.
 1. Defecation--Humor. 2. American wit and humor, Pictorial. I. Title.
PN6231.D37Y68 2010
818'.602--dc22

                        2009049929

        Printed and bound in the United States of America.

                SB 10 9 8 7 6 5 4 3 2 1

Contents

Acknowledgments vii

Introduction ix

Solo.................................... 1

The Gold Standard 3

The Thinker 4

90 Degrees............................. 7

The Lotus 8

The Reverse........................... 11

The Breast Exam 12

The Airplane Crash 15

Spread Eagle 16

The Torpedo 19

The Pike 20

The Crab 23

The Cannonball........................ 24

Frisk 27

Naked 28
The Butterfly. 31
Runner's Poop. 32
Poolside. 35
Skydive. 36
The Captain. 39
The Pommel Horse 40
One Cheek Lean. 43
Leapfrog 44
Doggystyle 47
High Crouch 48
Missionary Position. 51

Group Positions 53
Wedding Night. 55
Foot Massage. 56
Wheelbarrow 59
The Reverse Heimlich 60
The Cheerleader 63

Positions with Toys 65

Guitar 67

Kitty Style. 68

Brooklyn Style 71

Your Dad's Position. .72

Heroin (Mr. Brownstone). 75

The Foodie 76

Weight Lifting 79

The Giga-Flop 80

The Writer 83

Phone Poop. 84

The New York Breakfast 87

Gas Mask. 88

Specialty Positions 91

Public Toilet 93

In the Dark 94

Camping 97

Port-o-Poop. 98

Outhouse. 101

The Mile High Club. 102

Mirrors 105

A Poop Abroad 106

Aromatherapy. 109

Tantric 110

Conclusion. 113

About the Author 115

Acknowledgments

Without the following people, the *Kama Pootra* would have remained an arcane hobby for hardcore bathroom enthusiasts. I, along with the general public, owe them profound gratitude:

The folks at Sourcebooks; my agent Kristina Holmes at Ebeling & Associates; Dan "Radish" Aguilar, who brought to life my toilet muses: Ann Cho, Chris Larsen, Rita Okusako, and Tien Tran. Many thanks to these friends for pushing me along the way: Bharat Kumar Badhan, Joe Conte, Vicky Fong, and Kevin Liu.

Introduction

The average human performs approximately 25,000 bowel movements in his lifetime. Sadly, most people never depart from the first poop position they were taught as children. However, there exists another way, as you're about to learn. This book is the first adaptation of an ancient manual unearthed near the site of the first modern plumbing system. Believed to be written by a secretive monk order, the original writings and illustrations, which were inscribed on primitive toilet paper in a previously unknown dialect of Sanskrit, required five years of meticulous translation. Now for the first time in modern history, the *Kama Pootra*'s techniques and life directives are accessible to the pooping masses.

So what is it? The *Kama Pootra* is the authoritative educational guide for a new and exciting pooping experience, a governing handbook of free-thinking bathroom conduct. A combination of Dionysian excess and

Victorian modesty, the *Kama Pootra* offers a thrilling rediscovery of bathroom life. Within these pages, students will find new positions for home or work, alone or with friends, with or without the use of common household items. These lessons are the first step on the tiled path to an enlightened bathroom experience.

The first truth of the *Kama Pootra* is recognizing that self-discovery begins in the bathroom, where we are most vulnerable physically and emotionally. This book should serve as a guide, reference, and devotional as you walk through life as a student of the *Kama Pootra*. The second truth is that this must be an ongoing study. The *Kama Pootra* can never be mastered; you must strive for a life of constant improvement, never content with the ability to bring matter into the world merely as you have done before.

Despite our common literature, every student experiences the *Kama Pootra* in a personal manner. It is impossible to describe what you will feel; no human language possesses the vocabulary to accurately describe the sensations and body response to the *Kama Pootra*. Like snowflakes, each of our creations is unique, an intricate combination of genetics, lifestyle, and recent gastronomic intake.

The *Kama Pootra* mentions four types of bottoms: "doe," "cow," "water buffalo," and "elephant." Does and cows can be more adventurous in their congress with the toilet, while water buffalo and elephants are hampered by their very configuration and should proceed with caution when attempting some of the more difficult positions.

Every time the bathroom door closes, and you begin the sacred ritual again, an entirely new experience awaits.

Let's begin.

Solo

The *Kama Pootra* begins as a personal study of reflection and meditation. Before one can understand the *Kama Pootra*, he must possess an open mind freed from any preconceived notions about bathroom behavior.

The positions presented in this chapter are intended for the student alone. To begin, familiarize yourself with your surroundings: the coolness of a porcelain toilet, the contours of a tiled floor, the silken touch of toilet paper. Survey your anatomy with a close examination of what Arthur Rimbaud, the nineteenth-century French poet, referred to as the "enticing olive."* If you have never seen yourself in stark detail, try crouching over a carefully angled hand mirror.

Once you have an understanding of your body type and anatomy, you may begin to try the basic positions of the *Kama Pootra*. It is certain that some of these tasks may be uncomfortable at first, but remember that hard work is always plentifully rewarded in the bathroom.

*"Sonnet du trou du cul" or "Sonnet of the Asshole," A. Rimbaud (1873)

The Gold Standard

The Gold Standard is the foundation for all poop studies included in this book. When boys and girls enter into bathroom maturity—a good number by age three and some prodigious children as early as six months—this basic position is the first pose taught in Western toilet-centric cultures. It is remarkable for its simplicity and undemanding physical nature.

A famous Zimbabwean proverb stipulates, "If you can speak, you can sing. If you can walk, you can dance." Likewise: if you can sit, you can poop.

The Thinker

This is the premier position for deep contemplation. Many of the great philosophers in history used bathroom time to formulate theories about human nature. Take time to ponder life's greatest questions:

- What is the source of my happiness?

- Am I eating healthy enough?

- When did I eat so much corn?

90 Degrees

This position utilizes the full curvature of the toilet seat for a more well-rounded experience. Students with larger bottoms (water buffalo or elephants) will find that the 90 Degrees position is more comfortable because additional width is afforded by sitting perpendicular. This position is also useful for unsecured restrooms in that it allows greater options to observe the door directly.

The Lotus

This position is achieved by intertwining the legs upon the toilet seat to gain what the maharishis call "toilet levitation." The Lotus position is an excellent way to meditate and release the stresses and anxieties that build up from a modern caloric intake. Meditation in concert with a full release can elevate the consciousness to a plane approaching bathroom nirvana.

The Reverse

The Reverse position offers the student a new perspective of the bathroom, a 180, if you will, from the traditional positions of the *Kama Pootra*. By simply turning around from the standard position, the back is given a free range of motion should the student need to lean back or contort herself. From this position one can assume complete control of the toilet. A "drop and flush" maneuver can be completed in one fluid motion as the toilet is brought under quick and easy control.

The Breast Exam

An important aspect of the *Kama Pootra* is maintaining a healthy body. The *Kama Pootra* views the physical body as a sacred poop vault that must not be neglected. Harboring toxins and illness impairs the ability to harness maximum pleasure from a healthy poop experience. Maintaining a clean lifestyle and routinely performing self-screenings are simple proactive ways to retain the *Kama Pootra*'s full potential. While the most dangerous foe of the *Kama Pootra* is no doubt colon cancer, women should use this position at least once a month to check for unexpected lumps and hard masses. Your next poop may save your life.

The Airplane Crash

This position is fashioned after the airplane safety manual, which—in the event of a crash—advises that the head should be placed between the legs, arms interlocked under the knees. If needed, grab your ankles for leverage as you anxiously proceed in making a water landing.

Spread Eagle

Students blessed with preternatural flexibility can poop in positions most would never dare attempt. Like Leonardo's *Vitruvian Man*, the toilet Spread Eagle is an unforgettable image showcasing man's natural beauty. If you are prepared to spend long hours prostrating yourself for the sake of poop, this position is an attainable goal. Many of the devout have chosen this position as their life's work, a noble and worthwhile quest that demonstrates man striving to reach his potential.

The Torpedo

Although it is plentiful, toilet water is a vastly under-utilized resource. Its healing powers renew, refresh, and cleanse the bathroom soul. To release the torpedo, simply take repose in the cool calm waters and release after your bottom is completely submerged.

The Pike

This position brings the grace and elegance of Olympic diving directly to the bathroom. The Pike is initiated by imagining yourself as an Olympic diver, full of nerves in anticipation of a forthcoming plunge. Link your hands under extended legs, lower your head to your knees, and squeeze. Highest marks are achieved by minimizing the splash.

The Crab

When the *Kama Pootra* was first written, humans had a much closer relationship with nature and the animal kingdom. At the time, most people lived an agrarian lifestyle where they could closely observe the daily digestive habits of the livestock and surrounding wildlife. It was a natural conclusion that man began to imitate the way his animals gave their offerings to the Earth. Imitate the ways of the crab by facing upward upon the toilet supported by all fours, while using the legs and arms to suspend the bottom above the seat.

The Cannonball

After years of scientific tests and extensive 3-D computer simulations, a consensus was reached that this position provides maximum splash capability. By drawing the knees to the chest and applying inward pressure, latent bowel energy is forcefully released like a slingshot. The resulting splash is a refreshing treat that both cools and calms.

Frisk

Pooping is anaerobic exercise that puts high levels of stress on the lungs to quickly deliver oxygen to the bloodstream. With this simple physiology in mind, this position was designed for achieving maximum oxygen intake while pooping. When you position your hands on your head, the lungs are stretched so that air can be drawn deepest. Never again will you have to worry about hyperventilating and passing out on the toilet.

Naked

Man as he was designed, freed from the cloth to hide his shame. A return to Eden, if you will. To get the most out of this transcendent position, try the following. Upon entering the bathroom, face the toilet and slowly undress. Take extra time in unbuttoning your shirt and trousers—there is no need to rush. When you have liberated your body from garments and footwear, you may mount the porcelain throne. As the urges build, focus on the moment, trying to feel everything: the air, the floor, the toilet. Sacrifice yourself to the experience, release your inhibitions, and let everything go.

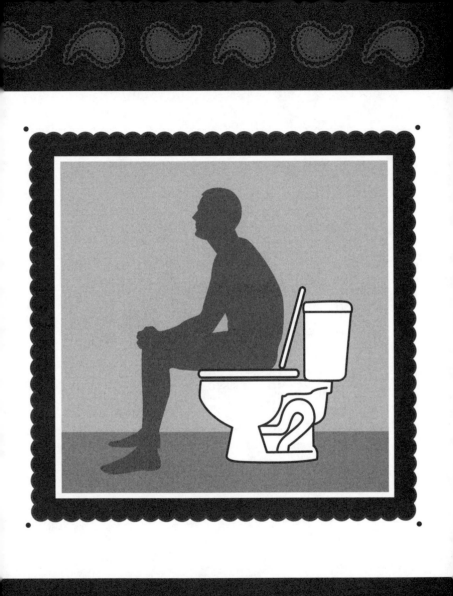

The Butterfly

Maintaining flexibility in the lower half of the body allows digestive chi to flow unencumbered through the limbs and outward to the toilet. This position, The Butterfly, puts emphasis on the two most important regions of the *Kama Pootra* chi: the groin and buttocks. In order to fully execute this position, grab your feet while squeezing your legs toward the toilet seat. After practicing this stretch for no less than twenty minutes, you may release.

Runner's Poop

Exercise biologists have proven that athletic potential has a direct relationship to an athlete's recent bowel activity. If you want to run your best, you must adequately prepare. This means carbo-loading—ingesting a high intake of carbohydrates the night before a race—and carbo-unloading minutes just before racing. This position addresses two critical preparations: a good stretch and a full purging of the colon. Why carry extra weight when it's not necessary?

Poolside

During the suburban sprawl of the '50s and '60s, every family yearned for two specific amenities for their tract homes: a swimming pool, and an outdoor toilet. This is the good life: a man sitting outdoors, on his toilet, tanning his entire front side. This is a position to use when you need life to slow down a little. Sit back, relax, and take in the fresh air. Everyone needs a moment to stop and smell the proverbial roses, even when those roses are poop.

Skydive

Lying supine across the toilet seat, the arms and legs fall limp. Relax as best you can, releasing all tension in the limbs so they hang lifeless. Now imagine that you are falling through the sky while blood collects in your extremities. Properly visualized, the rush of falling can be so intense that you will lose all bowel control. Pooping with the sensation of imminent death is one of life's greatest thrills.

The Captain

After a long night of eating and drinking, the body will want to expel all of the debris and poison infused into the digestive tract. The morning-after poop—or hangover poop—is the only position of the *Kama Pootra* that is permitted while under the influence of alcohol. This sobering purge brings closure to the previous night's festivities while renewing the poop lifecycle. In this position, Bacchus and Feechus, the gods of wine and poop respectively, are honored together.

The Pommel Horse

This pose takes its name from the beautiful yet demanding gymnastic discipline. In traditionally communist countries, children who show an early aptitude for the toilet are selected for government-sponsored athletic camps. Studies have shown that the toilet and the gymnastics apparatus require many of the same skills. This position exemplifies balance, arm strength, and finely tuned bowel control: universal characteristics of a world-class athlete.

One Cheek Lean

Beginning students of the *Kama Pootra* are surprised to learn that, like hands and eyes, humans have innate preference for one buttock. For sitting, the majority of the population is genetically right-buttocked; personality studies have shown this group to be more analytical but less creative with respect to bathroom behavior. Note: if you perform the One Cheek Lean on the nondominant buttock, this technique is known as The Stranger.

Leapfrog

This position requires leg flexibility and back strength, both of which should develop within months of starting the *Kama Pootra*. Position yourself into the Leapfrog pose by locking your legs at the rear of the seat and gripping the toilet with both hands in front of you. Arch your back and gaze to the ceiling while lowering the bottom to rest inches above the seat. After your body is shaped into this majestic pose, you may give your offering to the sacred pool.

Doggystyle

This unconventional position was traditionally regarded as uncivilized and untoward until the late 1960s. During a decade that deconstructed many oppressive social norms—the draft, the glass ceiling, and racial discrimination—poop liberation stands out as a shining accomplishment. The new attitudes toward pooping threw open the bathroom doors for the masses. Contemporary philosophers posited that if we are bound to pooping by natural law, we should own the method. Thus, Doggystyle is amoral, not immoral, and no better or worse than the *Kama Pootra*'s Gold Standard.

High Crouch

This position is ideal for the daredevil and the obsessively compulsive germaphobe. If you are the type of person who fears an invasion of toilet microbes, there is no other position in the *Kama Pootra* that keeps the sanitized buttocks farther away from the toilet seat. Standing tall on the seat requires exceptional balance, and should not be undertaken by those susceptible to spells of vertigo. After mounting the toilet and establishing a safe footing, bend ever so slightly to ensure a safe drop. Here the legs and spine are in a natural vertical alignment that prevents the intestinal crowding of sitting and provides an optimized exit point.

49

Missionary Position

Missionaries came to the New World with a royal mandate to teach civility, religion, and bathroom etiquette. Upon arrival, the colonists were appalled by the barbarity of the indigenous peoples' pooping methods, some of which included animal sacrifices and blood rituals. Gradually a new culture was imparted upon the natives and the culture of savage pooping was relegated to history books. This position took the moniker of Missionary Position because it was the only official position sanctioned for godliness by church authorities.

Group Positions

Pooping with a partner, or partners (sometimes referred to as group poop or gang pooping) produces a profound bond unattainable through team sports, the military, or marriage. This chapter explores the positions one can undertake with a lover, mentor, trusted friend, or relative. With a partner, you are able to share and address the deepest desires buried in your soul. These positions explore all combinations and permutations for a like-minded group. Whether you enter a monogamous relationship or choose to have many partners, the level of intimacy found within a shared bathroom is unparalleled. Because how can you really know someone unless you've pooped together?

His   Hers

Wedding Night

After the vows, the cake, the party, and the awkward sex, the real wedding night festivities can begin. Imagine: a newly wedded husband carrying his wife across the bedroom, past the bed, and into the bathroom—it is the apex of romance. The first poop as a married couple is an important ritual in the service of fully consummating the marriage. However, the first moments together in the bathroom can be both exciting and frightening. For couples who have abstained from premarital poop, there will be a natural awkwardness because both partners will be learning the act together. These couples should not be discouraged; sharing the *Kama Pootra* together is guaranteed to create a strong foundation to support a marriage.

Foot Massage

Like pooping, a bathroom foot massage is a delightfully intimate act. This position relieves stress in the regions that are most impacted throughout the workday: the feet and buttocks. Keeping these body parts relaxed is important to maintain low blood pressure and good colon health. Perform this position by having a partner knead out your feet's tension while you expel the remaining toxins collected in your abdomen.

Wheelbarrow

This position is designed for bathroom sweethearts. The lifter is to hold each of his partner's legs and elevate them per the sitter's instructions to raise, lower, or pause. It is important for the partners to remain in sync with each other by maintaining good communication and keeping eye contact throughout. This position is excellent for newlyweds to bond by working together toward a common goal: the perfect poop.

The Reverse Heimlich

Dr. Henry Heimlich invented his eponymous maneuver to quickly eject trapped objects by applying pressure to key regions of the abdomen. When the Heimlich maneuver was conceived, the doctor could not have known that two thousand years prior, the inventors of the *Kama Pootra* had devised a near identical technique. The only difference between the maneuvers is their objectives: The Reverse Heimlich was created for ejecting trapped and troublesome poop. To perform The Reverse Heimlich, lift your partner at the knees and aggressively pull toward the chest. If performed properly, the troublesome poop—or "devil's stones" in the literal Sanskrit—should be dramatically evacuated.

The Cheerleader

This is an excellent position for building trust between partners. The woman is instructed to sit idly upon the man's shoulders as he does his best to remain balanced while denying the normal muscle spasms and shaking of intestinal voiding. The partnership must move together and communicate to prevent a disastrous bathroom fall, in which points are deducted for an early dismount. Injuries—which often occur when attempting difficult new positions—can be prevented by practicing "safe poop": helmets, body pads, and a cushioned bathroom floor.

Positions with Toys

Throughout the ages, humans have searched for ways to enhance the bathroom experience with the help of physical instruments. The positions in this chapter demonstrate exactly what can be brought into the bathroom to amplify enjoyment and output. A poop toy by definition is any object brought into the bathroom: electronics, animals, and musical instruments are some examples. Poop toys should be used liberally and creatively—the possibilities are infinite.

Guitar

Music, language, the ability to wipe—these are the defining elements of humanity that set us apart from other animals. Music is the universal intermediary between the spiritual and material worlds. Music can be a vehicle to express all the pains and joys we experience in the bathroom. Everyone has musical talent buried within the bowels, though it can take time to reach its full expression. Songwriters throughout history entered the bathroom with nothing but a bellyful of writer's block and left with a melody bestowed by bathroom spirits.

Kitty Style

Pooping with animals is considered taboo in many world cultures. Regardless, it remains an edgy form of bowel expression that is actually augmented by its social prohibition. Despite its illegality in forty-eight states—Alabama and Massachusetts remain progressive with respect to human-animal bathroom relations—pooping with a furry friend has a significant cult following across the United States. This position is not as simple as one might assume; taking your pet into the bathroom is an acquired skill. Most pets, cats especially, have an aversion to pools of water and will need conditioning to calmly approach the toilet. You will find that well-groomed pets add warmth and a soothing touch to a bare lap.

Brooklyn Style

Hip hop music and culture, which originated in the early 1970s as a popular New York City counterculture movement, resonated deeply with New York City's youth. These artistic pioneers were looking for new ways of personal expression in the bathroom within the context of a culture they owned, and the hip hop commode became a raucous den of rhythm and improvisation. This position is fully equipped with bowel loosening bass grooves, as depicted here.

Your Dad's Position

For dads, pooping is a cherished rite. Being a dad means yardwork, nagging, and countless other uncelebrated duties, from which the bathroom is the only respite. The silent chamber is perhaps the only place where a man can truly be alone with his thoughts, a toilet oasis in a desert of familial responsibility, the last vestige of personal privacy. This position is a tribute to the fathers of the world who could use a fifteen-minute break alone with their thoughts and the newspaper.

Heroin (Mr. Brownstone)

Mixing drugs and pooping is living dangerously on the edge of the seat. This toilet thrill ride reached epidemic levels among Scottish youths in the early 1990s, which was later depicted in a critically acclaimed film. The following monologue served as the protagonist's call for understanding that pooping has its limits: "Choose poop. Choose a fine porcelain toilet. Choose a four bathroom suburban house in a sleepy suburban cul-de-sac. Choose four-ply toilet paper with a quaint geometric pattern. Choose a high-powered bidet with adjustable water temperature. Choose a nine-to-five job with hour-long bathroom breaks. Choose a wife who understands pooping is more important to you than she can ever be. Choose growing old and losing the bodily control you spent decades mastering. Choose poop."

The Foodie

If Virginia Woolf had studied the *Kama Pootra*, she surely would have added pooping to this list when she wrote, "One cannot think well, love well, sleep well, if one has not dined well."* A well-balanced meal is critically important when preparing for colonic combustion. Simply restated, what you put in determines what you get out.

*"A Room of One's Own," V. Woolf (1929)

Weight Lifting

Pooping with high levels of adrenaline and an elevated heart rate can create the conditions ripe for the phenomenon known as a pooper's high. With weights in hand, flex your biceps repeatedly as you feel the urges beginning to develop and intensify. Sweat will soon consume your clothes and body—you will find it a slick lubricant allowing you to move around on the seat unfettered by friction. As the lactic acid begins to build in your arms, you will find yourself pushed to the limit of endurance. But keep going— the cocktail of endorphins from exercise and bowel-elimination is as potent as any pharmacological drug.

The Giga-Flop

This position is for the workaholic who is keen to apply advanced technologies to the pooping experience. When your two daily priorities are pooping and work, this position allows you to synergize the responsibilities to the boss and bowels. It's a blending of the cubicle and the stall into a multitasker's wildest dream.

The Writer

The *Kama Pootra* is capable of bringing out the very best in us, literally and artistically. It pushes the body and mind to the limits of creativity. The emotions experienced while pooping are wide ranging; tears of agony transition seamlessly to tears of joy. Use the toilet to harness the creative self in translating the bathroom experiences to the written word. A great novel or poem is brewing in all our bellies, waiting patiently to be extracted.

Phone Poop

There are innumerable reasons why every bathroom should include a traditional phone line. In fact, many hotels now accommodate their en-suites with phones just so that guests can remain intimate with their loved ones back home. If your steady partner cannot be with you, pooping together over the phone is the next best alternative.

Phone poop is an intimate word game that requires practice and patience. When played properly, the right words can ignite a fiery bodily response. But first you must develop an adequate vocabulary. You will need a collection of words and phrases to describe the things your partner cannot see and smell.

Suggested bathroom dirty talk should involve: the warmth of the seat, the condition of the toilet, and when its depths were last plunged.

The New York Breakfast

The East Coast developed a poop zeitgeist diametrically opposed from the relaxed pooping styles of the Californian surfers and beatniks. New Yorkers traditionally start the day with coffee and cigarettes; this is sometimes referred to as the New York breakfast. Conveniently, both of these breakfast staples are colodiasiacs—naturally occurring rear stimulants—that can amount to an explosive morning. You'll find the mix of nicotine and caffeine to be a powerfully combustible intestinal additive.

Gas Mask

The gas mask is a useful and important tool for encounters with a recently used bathroom. Unfortunately, "smelly seconds" is a fact of communal habitation and work. If the bathroom has not had time to recalibrate its aura, a gas mask can limit the intake of stagnant essences left over by a roommate or co-worker. If at all possible, try and allow for a full bathroom refractory period. Thirty minutes should be enough for the bathroom to renew its environment and to cool the toilet and toilet seat. If not, this pose should do.

Specialty Positions

It's very unlikely that you will be able to poop on your favorite toilet, during your optimal hour, for your entire life. Even if your daily schedule revolves around your internal poop clock (as is recommended), there will come times when you will be forced into a foreign poop situation. Accept that these situations are inevitable. We must face them with courage and humility because—as the bathroom proverb stipulates—sometimes the mysterious garden yields the most exquisite fruit. This chapter delves into unique applications of the *Kama Pootra* away from the home. The student must be prepared for planes, trains, and—adequately furnished—automobiles (e.g., an RV).

Public Toilet

Since its inception, the public toilet has stricken fear into the heart of man. The source of the anxiety is our innate worry over the unknown. We fear what lies beyond our centered perception of reality: death, the darkness, the upkeep of the toilet at the community pool. The *Kama Pootra* teaches us that we overcome our fears by facing them and then proceeding to poop on them. With this position comfortably in your repertoire, there will be no public bathroom (e.g., gas stations, stadiums, airports) too daunting.

In the Dark

Neurologists have proven that if you deprive the brain of one of the five senses, the fungible three-pound mass in your head will rewire itself to enhance the four senses that remain. Likewise, a darkened bathroom will elevate all senses unrelated to vision. For touch, the rear nerve endings will strongly feel the rubbing upon the seat. For hearing, the mellifluous sounds of your body's instrument are heard with previously hidden subtones in the high and low registers. And most importantly, the olfactory sense—the sense of smell—is heightened. You'll find yourself engrossed in an essence so rich and pungent you'd never think it was produced by your own biology.

Camping

Camping can be a valuable escape from the grind of the nine-to-five work week and its soulless fifteen-minute bathroom break. Taking a few days to poop and breathe in open spaces is a necessary step to recharge the soul. Voiding while you gaze into a panoramic vista is a refreshing departure from the sometimes claustrophobic four-walled bathroom. Plus, when you leave nature and return to twenty-first-century life, you'll take home a new appreciation of modern plumbing systems.

Port-o-Poop

The ability to relieve oneself confidently in a portable toilet is an important part of a dynamic pooping repertoire. And it's absolutely essential if you plan a career in construction or if you're a Renaissance faire enthusiast. To defeat the anxiety caused by the communal odors and encroaching lines, practice for the Port-o-Poop by applying traditional techniques of transcendental meditation. Picture yourself on your favorite toilet, perhaps the toilet of your childhood. Visualize the way it used to make you feel at peace. This mental escape routine will let you poop anywhere, anytime, on anything.

Outhouse

Human progress has been marked by technological innovations applied to daily life: the train and the automobile, the steamship and the airplane, the telegraph and the telephone, the outhouse and the bathroom. The Outhouse is one of the *Kama Pootra*'s "pooping in history" positions. Like Civil War enthusiasts, certain bowel-focused individuals love to role-play as characters in a life untouched by modernity. If that suits your fancy, the outhouse is a time machine to our American past, when men were men, and pooping was just a wooden box and a hole in the ground.

The Mile High Club

You may think you know what the mile high club is, because of today's sex-focused culture. However, most are unaware that the lewd version usurped the name from the real club. Membership to our club is granted after relieving one's bowels at thirty thousand feet on one of the most challenging toilets ever invented. Be aware that there are many pitfalls that can prevent entry into this esteemed group: unexpected air turbulence can constrict the abdomen, affecting performance; children are known to impatiently knock on the bathroom door, creating performance anxiety; and flight attendants routinely query passengers taking longer than thirty minutes. In order to successfully gain membership to the club, you will need to focus on expediently getting in and out of the bathroom.

Mirrors

Reflective glass in the bathroom is an excellent way to enhance the bowel experience. Try gazing into your eyes moments prior to release. Like Narcissus, you will be overcome by your own beauty. A fully mirrored bathroom also provides the perfect practice environment—similar to a ballet studio—allowing you to practice endlessly in order to correct any flaws in your technique.

A Poop Abroad

During the college years, many young adults travel to Europe to "find themselves." However, what they often find is a culture shock brought about by the lack of American-style bathrooms. For many, this is the first time they will have to poop without their parents. In anticipation of these bathrooms, this position should be practiced with other travel preparations, including acquiring a passport, buying traveler's checks, etc. If there is one phrase you should have memorized before landing, it is, naturally, "Where is the toilet?"

Aromatherapy

As one might assume, smells play a unique role in bathrooms. Experiments have shown they have the power to influence our moods, virility, and overall colonic health. Candles and essential oils are widely available instruments of aromatherapy that should be used to calibrate the ideal bathroom atmosphere. There is a smell to suit all occasions and personalities—cedar for a woman's delicate ways, bubblegum for a child's cherubic plops, cayenne pepper for highly volatile explosions, etc. Try experimenting with a variety of aromas until you find the one that tickles the nose, arouses the brain, and loosens the bowels.

Tantric

The universal principles of tantra are easily applied to the bathroom through the *Kama Pootra*. Tantric pooping is founded on the idea that abstaining from a daily release can produce a spectacular euphoria later in an explosion of stored life force. If you can sustain your colonic "chakras"—pockets of life energy within the bowels—they can be used to reach a oneness with ultimate consciousness.

Begin by storing the chakras for a day, then two, and then three. Most nonprofessional poopers will stop here, but a small number of devout practitioners can then build from a week, to a month, and eventually a year. The release of one year's worth of tantric energy has only been achieved by the most gifted and focused pupils. It should be noted that the tantric application of the *Kama Pootra* is controversial and is not endorsed by the medical community.

Conclusion

Pooping is central to our innate humanity, a divine gift to be accepted with graciousness and humility. The act of pooping is special for humans, because we are the only species that possesses self-awareness; only humans are bestowed with the potential of the *Kama Pootra*. Seeking an elevated consciousness through pooping is humanity's bond. At the precise moment when you poop, there are millions of others in the world passing through the same emotional bathroom cycle of apprehension, fear, strife, anger, struggle, relief, pride, admiration, reflection, and peace.

The *Kama Pootra* is art and science, yin and yang, soul and bowel harmoniously interwoven in a rhythmic dance. Congratulations: you now possess the knowledge and techniques to live an enlightened life of untold riches in the bathroom. From this day forward may you never again poop blind to the beauty and deaf to harmony of the tiled den. Graciously accept membership into this elite collective and commit yourself to this lifestyle.

The *Kama Pootra* is a lifelong endeavor; it will stay with you until your last breath. Remember that one must poop to live. As Cartesian philosophy teaches, if you poop, then you must exist.* Practice these techniques until they are ingested deep within your soul.

Bathroom time is precious. Poop every time as if it were your last.

*"Je poop donc je suis" or "I poop therefore I am," René Descartes, *Discourse on the Method* (1637)

About the Author

Daniel Cole Young is a native of Livermore, California. Daniel is a graduate of the University of California at Davis, where he earned degrees in computer science and French. He lives in Los Angeles.

Skydive

Lying supine across the toilet seat, the arms and legs fall limp. Relax as best you can, releasing all tension in the limbs so they hang lifeless. Now imagine that you are falling through the sky while blood collects in your extremities. Properly visualized, the rush of falling can be so intense that you will lose all bowel control. Pooping with the sensation of imminent death is one of life's greatest thrills.

Poolside

During the suburban sprawl of the '50s and '60s, every family yearned for two specific amenities for their tract homes: a swimming pool, and an outdoor toilet. This is the good life: a man sitting outdoors, on his toilet, tanning his entire front side. This is a position to use when you need life to slow down a little. Sit back, relax, and take in the fresh air. Everyone needs a moment to stop and smell the proverbial roses, even when those roses are poop.